IMAGES
of America

SAN PEDRO'S
CABRILLO BEACH

In the 1930s, Cabrillo Beach was an ideal location for weekend getaways for the citizens of Los Angeles to spend time frolicking and playing at the water's edge. In the distance is the Middle Reservation of the Fort MacArthur military base.

ON THE COVER: The Cabrillo Beach Polar Bears Club crowns their king and queen on New Year's Day every year. Right after the crowning ceremony, the king and queen lead a crowd into the chilly waters of Cabrillo Beach like King Marion Chuka (kneeling, front left) and Queen Trudie Logan (front right) did in 1959. (Courtesy of the Cabrillo Beach Polar Bears Club.)

IMAGES
of America

SAN PEDRO'S
CABRILLO BEACH

Mike Schaadt, Ed Mastro,
and Cabrillo Marine Aquarium

ARCADIA
PUBLISHING

Published by Arcadia Publishing
Charleston SC, Chicago IL, Portsmouth NH, San Francisco CA

Library of Congress Catalog Card Number: 2008933033

For all general information contact Arcadia Publishing at:
Telephone 843-853-2070
Fax 843-853-0044
E-mail sales@arcadiapublishing.com
For customer service and orders:
Toll-Free 1-888-313-2665

Visit us on the Internet at www.arcadiapublishing.com

To John M. and Muriel Olguin, who have spent their lives enjoying Cabrillo Beach and making it a great place for people to gather and enjoy the ocean.

CONTENTS

Acknowledgments   6

Introduction   7

1.   Making of Cabrillo Beach   9

2.   Cabrillo Beach Coastal Park   35

3.   Community Groups   57

4.   Lifeguards   71

5.   Cabrillo Marine Museum and Cabrillo Marine Aquarium   79

6.   Events   97

ACKNOWLEDGMENTS

This book would not be as full or as comprehensive as it is without the help of John M. and Muriel Olguin, Ray Falk, Bill and Mary Samaras, Clark Faulk Jr., Kim White, Anne Hansford of the San Pedro Historical Society, the Los Angeles Harbor Department, Gary Florin, the *Daily Breeze*, the Cabrillo Beach Polar Bears Club, Fort MacArthur Military Museum, the Los Angeles Maritime Museum, and the International Star Class Yacht Racing Association. These sources were extremely helpful in contributing images and information to supplement the many vintage photographs that appear in this book from the archives of the Cabrillo Marine Aquarium.

All author's proceeds from the sale of this publication will benefit the mission of the Cabrillo Marine Aquarium, which is to engage people in education, recreation, and research to promote the knowledge, appreciation, and conservation of the marine life of Southern California.

INTRODUCTION

Since its beginning in 1927, San Pedro's Cabrillo Beach has been a popular beach destination for residents of San Pedro as well as Los Angeles and all of Southern California. This beach is characterized by the blending of man-made features like the sandy shores on the harbor side and open ocean side of the breakwater with the rugged natural habitats of the Palos Verdes Peninsula all on the fringe of the Port of Los Angeles, one of the largest and busiest ports in the world. Cabrillo Beach is home to the historic bathhouse, Cabrillo Marine Aquarium, Point Fermin State Marine Park, a fishing pier, public boat launch, and youth sports center.

Many groups of people like the Cabrillo Beach Polar Bears Club, Cabrillo Beach Boosters, Los Angeles City and County Lifeguards, Recreation and Parks Department of the City of Los Angeles, and the Cabrillo Marine Aquarium have helped shape the personality of Cabrillo Beach over the years. Community events are seasonal at the beach. In winter, the Cabrillo Beach Polar Bears Club invites everyone to join them for their New Year's Day swim and crowning of the king and queen polar bears. Cabrillo Marine Aquarium welcomes people to join them in celebrating whales at the Cabrillo Beach Whale Fiesta. Together with the American Cetacean Society, Cabrillo Marine Aquarium provides trained naturalists on whale-watch boats, which ply the waters just off Cabrillo Beach, to see gray whales on their annual migration up and down the coast. In spring, there are celebrations for Earth Day, daily programs on the beach for schoolchildren to learn about the ocean, and Meet the Grunion Nights to view the spawning of the fish with unusual reproductive habits. Summer brings huge crowds of beachgoers, the Fourth of July celebration and fireworks display, windsurfing tournaments, and the San Pedro Battle of the Beach for junior lifeguards. Coastal Cleanup Day, Chocolate Lobster Dive, San Juan Days, and round-the-lighthouse swims take place in fall. Year-round activities at Cabrillo Beach over the years have included tide pool walks, community festivals, bodybuilding contests, Hollywood film shoots, bathing beauty contests, bird watching, beach cleanups, kayaking, snorkeling, scuba diving, boating, fishing, windsurfing, and jet skiing.

Some of the memorable individuals important to the history of Cabrillo Beach are Juan Rodriguez Cabrillo, the Portuguese or Spanish conquistador who is the namesake of Cabrillo Beach and the first European to explore the West Coast of what is now the United States; U.S. Sen. Stephen M. White, who led the fight to have a port in San Pedro that became the Port of Los Angeles; Dr. William Lloyd, the first director of the Cabrillo Marine Museum; and John M. Olguin, Los Angeles City Lifeguards captain at Cabrillo Beach, who was the second director of Cabrillo Marine Aquarium and was celebrated as San Pedro's "Citizen of the Century."

The rich history of Cabrillo Beach includes major events like the making of the breakwater in the early 1900s, the additions of the inner beach boathouse and the historic bathhouse in the 1930s, additions of a gun placement and bunker during World War II, the building of the fishing pier in 1969, the explosion of the tanker SS *Sansinea* in 1976, the opening of the "new" Cabrillo Marine Museum in 1981, many years of high surf from El Niño storms, the opening of the renovated historic bathhouse on its 70th anniversary in 2002, and the opening of the expansion to the Cabrillo Marine Aquarium in 2004.

Cabrillo Beach welcomes residents and visitors of Los Angeles and surrounding communities to enjoy one of Southern California's great beach areas.

One

MAKING OF
CABRILLO BEACH

The eastern point of the Palos Verdes Peninsula, which connects to San Pedro Harbor, was a rocky shore habitat in the late 1800s. In those days, before the creation of the Port of Los Angeles, the shoreline of San Pedro Harbor was a huge natural wetland. With the decision to develop the Port of Los Angeles in San Pedro and the building of what was then the largest breakwater in the world, another decision was made to create a beach on either side of the beginning of the breakwater. It was named Cabrillo Beach after Juan Rodriguez Cabrillo, the first European to sail up and down the coast of California.

The City of Los Angeles annexed San Pedro in 1925 and the maintenance, safety (in the form of lifeguards), and recreational programming became the responsibility of the City of Los Angeles Department of Playground and Recreation (later to be called the Recreation and Parks Department). A boathouse was built on the inner beach with a wooden pier and a bathhouse was constructed on the outer beach. Picnic pavilions called pergolas were built on the sand of the outer beach.

The federal government considered building a major port for Southern California in Santa Monica, Marina del Rey, and Redondo Beach as well as San Pedro. After much lobbying, San Pedro was selected. The government decided to build a breakwater to protect San Pedro Bay and the new world-class port. Construction began on the San Pedro Breakwater in 1899. The first 2-mile stretch was finished in 1912.

On April 26, 1899, President McKinley pressed a button in the library of the White House whereby the machinery was set in motion to fill the air chambers of this barge, causing it to roll over on one side and the rocks to tumble into the water. Unfortunately, the mechanism of the new barge failed to work, so the rocks had to be pushed off by hand. This was accepted as symbolic of the entire harbor undertaking—nothing about it had come easily. If not for tremendous individual and community efforts, it could have never been accomplished.

After the first rocks were dumped to start the breakwater, a large Free Harbor Jubilee celebration sponsored by the government was held that lasted two days. Twenty thousand people were in attendance. The following day a flower parade was held in Los Angeles celebrating the event.

Senator White

Sen. Stephen M. White was one of the honored guests at what is believed to be the first picnic at Cabrillo Beach.

The original breakwater was to be 8,500 feet long at a cost of $2.9 million. Pilings were driven out into the water 2.5 miles and a track laid on the pilings. The breakwater was built toward the shore and the tracks removed and the pilings cut off as the breakwater grew toward land.

The main channel and Terminal Island can be seen, before the breakwater was extended, in the background of this c. 1904 photograph. The foreground shows the flatcars of rock being transported from the Chatsworth Quarry in Chatsworth, California, to be used for the breakwater. Originally rocks for the breakwater were quarried from Santa Catalina Island, but due to multiple complications, a mainland source was chosen later in the project.

A shack was built to store tools at the beginning of the railway pier that was used to make the breakwater. The locomotive on the tracks would stop and workers would load or unload the hand tools needed for the day's work. This photograph was taken around 1888.

Some of the stones used in the breakwater weighed from 6,000 to 16,000 pounds each. They were arranged like steps with the heavier ones on the sea side. The breakwater was built like a flight of seven steps with 2-foot risers on the harbor side and four steps of 4-foot risers on the sea side.

BIRDS EYE VIEW OF TOWN AND WATER FRONT OF
SAN PEDRO

A drawing by the Los Angeles Harbor Department in 1905 shows an active main channel and an undeveloped Cabrillo Beach area in the upper left.

MARINA

In the 1950s, the Los Angeles Harbor Department included a plan for further development of the harbor that included plenty of dock space in and around Cabrillo Beach for the growing number of people moving into communities around Los Angeles.

Angel's Gate Lighthouse was built in 1913 and is located at the end of the San Pedro Breakwater. This lighthouse marks Angel's Gate, the main entrance to the Port of Los Angeles. This view is looking towards the harbor with the Palos Verdes Peninsula in the background.

Over the years, Angel's Gate Lighthouse has endured raging storms, mountainous waves, and at least one errant steamship that struck the jetty below. Besides a slight tilt, the lighthouse has survived this type of treacherous weather, as well as the accidents, unscathed. The lighthouse was automated in 1973, thus eliminating the need for keepers. Mariners entering Angel's Gate are guided by the lighthouse's rotating green light, which is the only green light in a lighthouse along the West Coast. This view is looking south towards the San Pedro Channel.

There was a pier, called the Navy Pier, where the current youth base is now located. It was used by the U.S. Navy to shuttle sailors from their ships to shore and as a place for smaller shore boats to tie up to. Sailors used the pier to get to the middle reservation of Fort MacArthur where Trona Field featured ball fields and later a gym for boxing and recreation.

People would park at the top of the cliffs for a day at the shore near Point Fermin before the making of Cabrillo Beach.

Before the addition of sand in 1927, the ocean went right up to the cliffs as seen in this 1924 photograph taken from the new San Pedro Breakwater.

The outer beach had a small village near the shore end of the newly completed San Pedro Breakwater. This picture is from May 7, 1925, before the addition of sand.

In 1913, Capt. John Barneson, founder of General Petroleum, was instrumental in building an oil pipeline from the Midway oil fields in Kern County to Los Angeles and eventually to San Pedro Bay. The pipeline terminated at a dock located along the bay side of the newly completed San Pedro Breakwater. Ships would fill their holds with oil and transport it to ports around the world. Captain Barneson was an influential figure in commerce and development on the California coast in the beginning of the 20th century. Interest in oil production stayed in the family as the life of Captain Barneson's son, Harold James Barneson, was the basis for the 2007 movie *There Will Be Blood*.

Helen Sower's house was built in the winter of 1924. The Sower family moved in to this house in 1925, and it was one of the few family residences right on Cabrillo Beach.

Wood embankments visible in this 1927 photograph were used to keep boulders in place as sand was added to outer Cabrillo Beach.

After the completion of the breakwater, Cabrillo Beach was created by adding sand from harbor dredging in 1927.

The addition of sand to the inner beach resulted in a wide expanse of land where later improvements would add parking and recreation facilities.

The result of the added sand in 1927 was a new, expansive outer beach. During the spring of 1928, Dr. Francis Clark of the California Department of Fish and Game observed the first grunion run on Cabrillo Beach.

After Cabrillo Beach opened, residents in San Pedro, Wilmington, Los Angeles, and other surrounding cities flocked to enjoy the new sandy beach. These bathing beauties are members of Job's Daughters International, an organization of young women between the ages of 10 and 20 who are related to a Master Mason. They pose for a photograph on June 4, 1927.

These girls enjoy the first day the new Cabrillo Beach opened to the public in 1928. San Pedro city leaders were anxious to have a destination for visitors and residents to enjoy the beach.

In this 1928 picture of the new Cabrillo Beach, the boathouse and pier already exist on inner Cabrillo Beach. The boathouse provided a place for people to rent beach gear and boats.

In 1931, this front view facing south of the bathhouse can be seen while still under construction on outer Cabrillo Beach.

There is only sand around the Cabrillo Beach Bathhouse that is still under construction in this 1931 photograph looking from the outer beach side. It opened to the public in 1932. The bathhouse was part of the preparation for the 1932 Los Angeles Olympic Games. The boathouse also served as a venue for sailing events held in the harbor.

Residents on the cliffs above Cabrillo Beach have a great view of the bathhouse, boathouse, San Pedro Bay, and the Port of Los Angeles.

The boathouse offered a hub of activity for people enjoying the calm inner Cabrillo Beach. Horseshoe pits can be seen in the lower left of the image and are just one of the various recreational activities offered at Cabrillo Beach. By 1932, the outer beach had the new bathhouse. Beachgoers

would take the Pacific Red Car to the beach, rent a towel at the bathhouse, and spend the day enjoying the surf and sand. The bathhouse was declared a historical landmark in 1989.

Sewage from Cabrillo Beach was transported by pipeline to San Pedro and then on to Terminal Island for disposal. The Sower House and the cliffs can be seen in the background.

The filled area on inner Cabrillo Beach was paved from the foot of the cliffs to the sand. The popularity of Cabrillo Beach is evident by the full parking lot in this 1930s photograph.

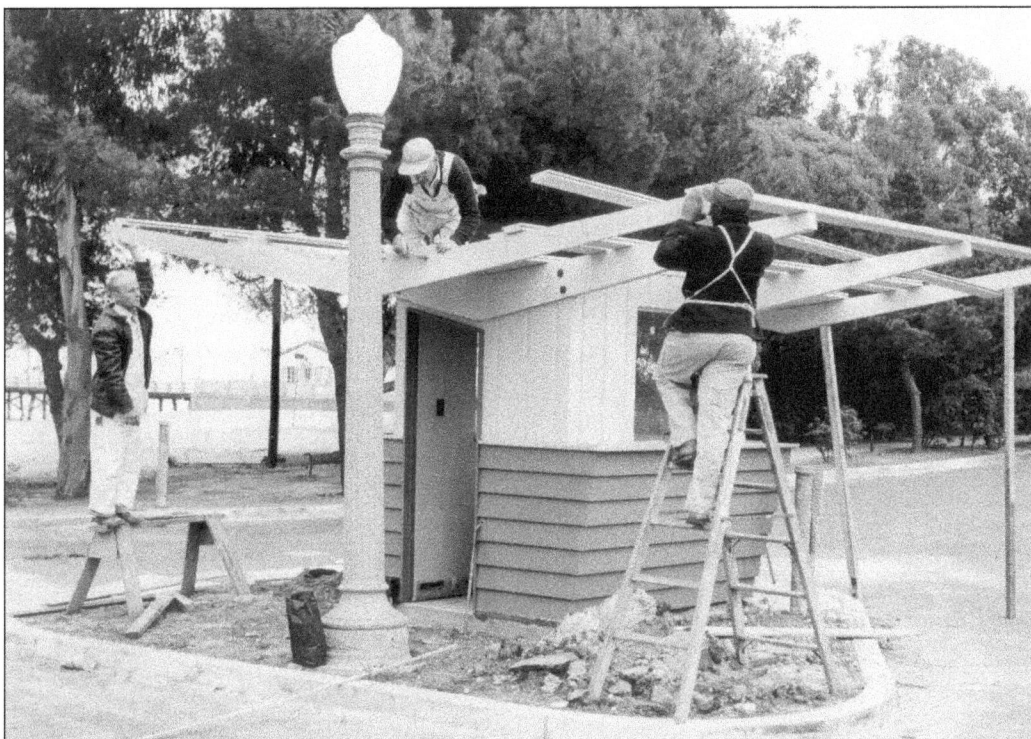

Builders put the finishing touches on a new parking booth in April 1952. The City of Los Angeles collects parking fees to offset the cost of maintaining a clean and safe beach for recreational and educational programs.

People enjoy the inner beach on June 29, 1935. The boathouse was a center of activity on the inner beach with people walking along the pier and talking with the lifeguards stationed at lifeguard headquarters.

A beach groomer sifts through the sand at Cabrillo Beach to keep it clean and safe. The City of Los Angeles has provided maintenance and recreational programs since the creation of the beach.

The boathouse in this December 1955 photograph shows the pilings that it and the pier were built upon. In addition to renting beach gear and boats, it also served as a lifeguard tower and headquarters for Los Angeles City Lifeguards.

Constant erosion in the sand around the base of the boathouse eventually led to its demolition in the 1970s.

Women relax on the first Jeep used by Los Angeles City Lifeguards at Cabrillo Beach during a Recreation and Parks–sponsored Camera Day. This Jeep was procured by John M. Olguin from a Los Angeles Fire City Department surplus yard and was made to work and look like new by using donations obtained from the community.

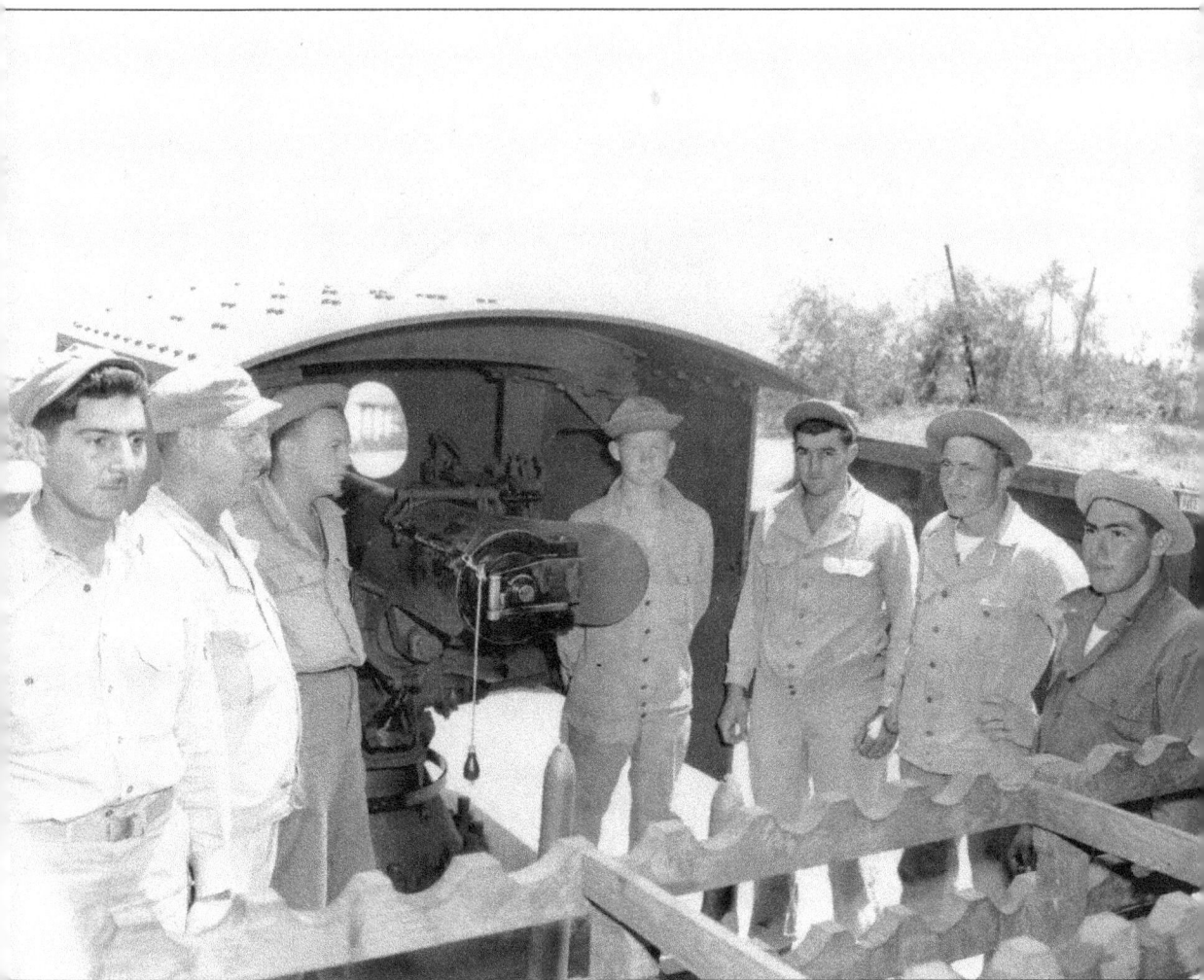

During World War II, security of the Los Angeles Harbor increased due to the fear of being attacked. A gun emplacement was built in 1943 on the bluff near the entrance to Cabrillo Beach as part of the coastal defenses used at Los Angeles Harbor.

600.919 (Los Angeles) CM 41772

REPORT OF COMPLETED WORKS - SEACOAST FORTIFICATIONS
(Batteries)   GUNS 1 + 2 FROM
                        BATTERY
                        LODOR

SPEKM-1.

HARBOR DEFENSES OF LOS ANGELES
FORT MAC ARTHUR (CABRILLO BEACH)
BATTERY JAAN - No. 1   No. of guns 2
CALIBER 3-INCH R.F.   CARRIAGE PEDESTAL

Part I   Corrected to 27 November 1943

GENERAL:
  Battery commenced: 6 July 1942
  Battery completed: 11 January 1943
  Date of transfer: 12 April 1943
  Cost to date of transfer: $8040.11
  Materials of construction: Reinforced Concrete
  Battery new or modernized: New

  Trunnion elevation in battery: No.1: 44.5'; No.2: 43.5'
  Datum plane: Mean Lower Low Water

UTILITIES:
  WATER SUPPLY
  Source of: Municipal Service
  Alternate source: None
  Size of main: 1-inch (Extended from troop housing)
SEWER:
  Connected to sewer: No
  Type of disposal: None
  Type of latrine: None

UTILITIES: (Contd.)
ELECTRIC POWER
  Sources of: See "Remarks"-1"
  Procured & installed by: OCE
  Characteristics: Voltage 110 AC Single Phase 60 Cycle
  Max. K.W. required for utilities: 1 KW
  Max. K.W. required for nonbattle conditions: 3 KW
  Commercial power provided: Yes   Capacity: 5 KW
  Auxiliary power unit provided: No   Capacity: - -
  Type of lighting fixtures: V.P. in magazines, balance oper
  Dehumidifying unit: Make and capacity: None
  Rooms wet or dry: Dry
  How ventilated: Not ventilated
  How heated: Not heated
DATA TRANSMISSION:
  Type: Battery Field Telephone - Type EE-91 RCA Teletal
        System - 110 V.
REMARKS:
  1. Public Utilities (Bureau of Power & Light, City of L.A.)
     (Lighting Magazines)
  2. Origin of Coordinates: Station "R" (U.S.C. & G.S. Static
     "Deadman's Island")

ARMAMENT

Emplacement Number	Cal.	Length	Guns Model	Serial No.	Manufacturer	Mounted	Type	Model	Carriages Serial No.	Manufacturer	Motor
1	3 "	50 Cals.	1903 15Pdr.	105	Watervliet	Yes	Pedestal	1903	105	Watervliet	None
2	3 "	"	"	106	"	"	"	"	106	"	"

FS-513 Prin Card 29   CONFIDENTIAL

This is the report for the completed work of the gun battery at Cabrillo Beach that was part of the harbor defenses of Los Angeles and Fort MacArthur. The emplacement was completed in 1943.

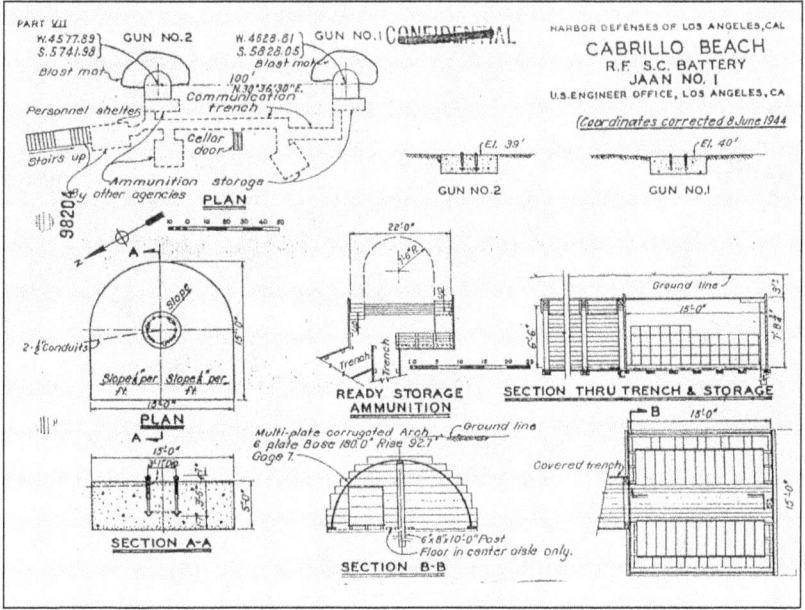

The plans for the gun battery included reinforced cement and two guns. The placement of this gun battery afforded protection of Angel's Gate.

Over the years, the Army Corps of Engineers has arranged for replenishment of the sand at Cabrillo Beach like the project completed in fall and winter of 1991.

Sand is transported by winter storm waves away from the beach and deposited back onto the beach in the summer. However, there is also a long shore current that pulls the sand taken from the beach south along the coast. The Palos Verdes Peninsula is a poor source of sand. Sand scoured by winter waves on man-made Cabrillo Beach is not all replaced during the summer, resulting in a net loss of sand every year.

Rocks were again added to the San Pedro Breakwater in the mid-1960s. This time the rocks were piled on the eastern side of the outer beach perpendicular to the breakwater.

The Army Corps of Engineers built this groin to reduce sand erosion at Cabrillo Beach and to lengthen the time between beach sand–replenishment projects.

In this November 1926 picture of the beginning of the breakwater, the first segment of the San Pedro Breakwater is complete. The beach was to be built the next year.

Before Cabrillo Beach existed, visitors to the shore walked down a trail to the shallow tide pools of Point Fermin. This picture is from April 1923.

Two

CABRILLO BEACH COASTAL PARK

No other oceanfront in metropolitan Los Angeles offers the range of recreational opportunities and seashore habitats as that of Cabrillo Beach. And all are within easy walking distance. There is a rocky shore with tide pools, near-shore kelp beds, a wave-swept outer beach, calm inner beach, rocky breakwater, fishing pier, man-made salt marsh, public boat launch, native plant garden, fossil-rich cliffs, public aquarium, bathhouse, picnic facilities, and in the past a boathouse.

Recreational opportunities like playground equipment for children, volleyball courts, and horseshoe pits right on the sand make Cabrillo Beach a destination for families. Throughout the history of Cabrillo Beach, visitors have been reminded of Los Angeles Harbor's past with statues and artifacts from ships that include anchors, bells, and even a capstan.

In this view from the end of the pier of the boathouse, houses can be seen on the cliffs above

inner Cabrillo Beach.

Some of the early play equipment included these swings on outer Cabrillo Beach. The Port of Los Angeles Warehouse 1 can be seen in the background of this picture.

On a clear day, people using the swings on outer Cabrillo Beach can look south and see Catalina Island just 24 miles across the San Pedro Channel.

Many different play structures have been on Cabrillo Beach, including these installed on the inner beach in the mid-1990s that were made from recycled plastic materials.

With umbrellas dotting the oceanfront, beachgoers relax on inner Cabrillo Beach. In the background is the lower reservation of Fort MacArthur. The peaks in the haze are the San Gabriel Mountains.

People pulled trailers holding their boats down to the sand on inner Cabrillo Beach and launched their boats into San Pedro Bay. Fisherman, water-skiers, and day sailors all enjoyed the ocean year-round.

The sand was a challenge for boaters to launch and recover their boats. Many times boaters found the wheels buried in the sand as they tried to drive their cars with heavy trailers back onto firm ground.

A public boat-launch ramp opened on the north end of inner Cabrillo Beach on March 27, 1980, to accommodate the growing number of boaters who were anxious to get their vessels safely in and out of the water at Cabrillo Beach. City of Los Angeles Lifeguards keep watch on activities at the boat-launch ramp from their adjacent tower.

When jet skis became popular in the 1980s, enthusiasts of them used the boat launch to get their crafts into the ocean.

41

Beachgoers not only enjoyed the new sand at Cabrillo Beach but also the view of the Pacific Ocean from the breakwater.

Anglers started fishing from the breakwater as soon as it was finished. In this picture taken July 6, 1935, the bathhouse can be seen on the right and Point Fermin on the left.

The pier at Cabrillo Beach was built in 1969. It is low and near the water and extends out 1,200 feet into San Pedro Harbor, running parallel to the breakwater. Prior to installing the pier, people would fish from the more treacherous breakwater and often get washed into the surf of the rising tide.

Local fishermen try their luck at the fishing pier to catch white croakers, Pacific mackerel, bonito, queenfish, sand bass, and halibut. The snack bar and bait shop was removed during a renovation in the late 1990s and replaced with a large covered outdoor seating area.

Renovations to the Cabrillo Beach Pier were done in the early 1990s. One of the major changes was the removal of the snack and bait shop, which was replaced by a large sturdy awning to provide shade to people relaxing on the pier. The groin on outer Cabrillo Beach can be seen in the foreground of this picture, and Angel's Gate lighthouse is in the background.

Some of the rocks used in the building of the San Pedro Breakwater were quarried from the southeastern end of Catalina Island. Two very large anchors were used to keep a barge holding the rocks in place off the coast of Catalina Island. After the operation ended, the anchors were donated and installed on Stephen M. White Drive by the Los Angeles Harbor Department.

The two anchors appeared to stand guard near the entrance to Cabrillo Beach in 1958. The San Pedro 30-Year Club dedicated the anchors, weighing 4 tons each, on November 24, 1957.

In 1989, the anchors were moved from Cabrillo Beach and set just east of the Mueller House, home to the San Pedro Historical Society. The statue of Sen. Stephen M. White replaced the two 4-ton anchors.

The 30-Year Club of San Pedro donated an anchor in memory of all mariners and to commemorate the opening of the Mariner's Exhibit at Cabrillo Marine Museum. Museum director Dr. W. H. Lloyd (left) was joined by, from left to right, Frank Perkens, Lucky Foote, and Dr. John Dimassa from the 30-Year Club of San Pedro on the day of dedication, September 28, 1951.

In 1908, a bigger-than-life bronze statue of Sen. Stephen M. White was placed in front of the Old County Courthouse at the corner of Temple Street and Broadway in downtown Los Angeles to honor him for his strong leadership in the struggle to create the Los Angeles Harbor in San Pedro as opposed to Santa Monica Bay. In 1989, the statue was finally moved to its current location at the entrance to Cabrillo Beach on Stephen M. White Drive.

The statue is the work of Douglas Tilden, who was one of the most prolific sculptors in California in the early 1900s. The statue replaced two 4-ton anchors used to create the San Pedro Breakwater that were moved to Harbor Boulevard and Cliff Drive in San Pedro.

A ship's bell was installed in front of the Cabrillo Marine Museum in 1956. John M. Olguin found the bell at a salvage yard. The bell was rung on special occasions such as the Fourth of July and could be heard throughout Cabrillo Beach. The bell was stolen a couple of years after installation.

The stolen bell was replaced by the bell from the USS *Los Angeles*. City of Los Angeles part-time staffers John Truta and Joe Anderson regularly cleaned and polished the ship's bell.

The bell from Cabrillo Beach was removed and installed outside the Los Angeles Maritime Museum in 1985. This bell was salvaged from the USS *Los Angeles* and joined many other artifacts around the Maritime Museum from that U.S. Navy heavy cruiser.

Sculptor Henry Lion made this 2-foot-high plaster model of Juan Rodriguez Cabrillo from which he made a final large model in clay. From the large clay model, a mold was made for the final sculpture to be cast in concrete.

The statue of Juan Rodriguez Cabrillo was dedicated in 1936. Sculptor Henry Lion is standing to the right of two unidentified City of Los Angeles Recreation and Parks representatives.

The hospital ship USS *Relief* (center) and the repair ship USS *Medusa* (right) sit at anchor just off the Los Angeles Breakwater in the late 1930s. The barge with the tall target structure at the left of the photograph was towed out to sea for gunnery practice.

The calm waters at the base of the boathouse attracted families to the shore. Many youngsters learned to swim here with the help of City of Los Angeles Lifeguards.

After a fun day at Cabrillo Beach, residents used a trail from outer Cabrillo Beach to gain access to their homes on top of the cliffs. Nonresidents packed up their towels and beach equipment, loaded up their cars, and made their way back home.

Bait barges like this one in the Los Angeles Harbor provide live anchovies and squid for sportfishing boats full of recreational fishermen on their way to the waters off Palos Verdes Peninsula and Catalina Island.

Angel's Gate Park is located at the top right of this photograph. Originally known as the upper reservation of Fort MacArthur, the property is now owned and operated by Los Angeles City Department of Recreation and Parks. Angel's Gate is home to the Fort MacArthur Military Museum, Forth MacArthur Marine Mammal Care Center, and the International Bird Rescue Center.

The rocky shore of Point Fermin on the western side of outer Cabrillo Beach offers beachgoers opportunities to observe Southern California marine life in tide pools. Man-made cement structures can be seen as people walk out to the tide pools. Catalina Island can be seen in the background.

The tide pools were very popular for people to investigate at low tide. The Cabrillo Marine Museum recruited and trained volunteers to help with the demand for tours of the tide pools. These volunteers, including Cabrillo Marine Museum volunteer president Barbara Beckler (center) and Nancy Carrigan (right), answered questions about intertidal animals and plants. The volunteers also warned people of the destruction caused by removing marine life from the tide pools. Despite valiant efforts by volunteers and Cabrillo Beach staff, people regularly took tide pool animals and plants home as souvenirs.

After many years of hard lobbying by groups such as the Cabrillo Marine Museum, led by director John M. Olguin, the tide pools at Point Fermin received the special designation of State Marine Life Refuge.

The opening of the Point Fermin Marine Life Refuge in December 1969 was cause for celebration. The Cabrillo Marine Museum welcomed the community to join in the celebration, which included a parade. Muriel Olguin made the colorful banners used in the parade.

The Port of Los Angeles built a 3.5-acre salt marsh in 1985 on the northern end of inner Cabrillo Beach to mitigate the disruption of natural habitat for some of their port expansion projects. An island was created on the northern end of the salt marsh for shorebirds to nest.

They named this man-made wetland Salinas de San Pedro and gave control of public access to the Cabrillo Marine Aquarium. Exhibits were added on the observation deck so visitors could learn more about this salt marsh and other wetlands in Southern California.

A fully accessible trail was added to allow visitors easy and safe access to the tide pools at Point Fermin from inner Cabrillo Beach. The $700,000 project was paid for by grants from the California State Coastal Conservancy, the City of Los Angeles, and Los Angeles County. At the ribbon-cutting ceremony in August 2000, from left to right, are an unidentified man; Los Angeles City councilman Rudy Svornich; City of Los Angeles, Department of Recreation and Parks general manager Ellen Oppenheim; unidentified; and Cabrillo Marine Aquarium director Dr. Susanne Lawrenz-Miller.

Three

COMMUNITY GROUPS

Cabrillo Beach was a popular gathering place for people even before the beach was created in 1928. Many Sunday drives ended with a picnic on the bluffs above the rocky tide pools. Fishermen fished from the shore, the breakwater, and later the groin on the outer beach, and the fishing pier on the inner beach.

Once the beach was completed and opened to the public in 1928, families came to enjoy lying on the sand and playing in the water. In the early 1930s, pergolas built on the outer beach were popular with groups for barbecues and parties until they fell into disrepair and were removed in the 1940s.

The reliable afternoon breeze led to the area off Cabrillo Beach called "Hurricane Gulch" and attracted day sailors, model yacht sailors, and windsurfers.

Swimmers often ended their channel swims from Catalina Island at Cabrillo Beach. Lifeguards, family, and friends would greet the exhausted swimmers that made the 25-mile crossing. Other swimming contests were held over the years like racing from the Angel's Gate Lighthouse to outer Cabrillo Beach or even racing around the lighthouse. These swims were sponsored by lifeguard groups, swimming federations, or the Cabrillo Beach Polar Bears Club.

Cabrillo Beach Polar Bears Club has been a very active group at Cabrillo Beach since being started by John M. Olguin and Jack Cheaney in 1946. The New Year's Day Swim at Cabrillo Beach is an annual event put on by the club. This popular community event had its start when youngsters, including John M. Olguin, Muriel (Groat) Olguin, and Ray Falk, all from the San Pedro Swim Club, first braved the winter water in 1936. Starting in 1952, a king and queen among the polar bears were selected to serve as goodwill ambassadors at polar bear events throughout the year, including leading the charge into the chilly waters of outer Cabrillo Beach at 12:00 p.m. on New Year's Day. The Cabrillo Beach Polar Bears Club joined the Cabrillo Beach Booster Club and the San Pedro Historical Society in the late 1990s to lead the fight to designate the Cabrillo Beach Bathhouse as a state historical structure and for its eventual renovation. The newly renovated bathhouse opened to the public in 2002, the 70th anniversary of its original opening.

Swimmers joined the second Cabrillo Beach Polar Bears Club New Year's Swim at Cabrillo Beach in 1953. All who went into the chilly seawater received a certificate to commemorate their feat.

The typewriter on the right of this photograph was used to type the name onto a certificate that each participant brought home. That year, the king was Raymond Person and the queen was Marguerite Gardiner.

In the early days of the Polar Bears Club Swim at Cabrillo Beach, only two to three dozen hearty people walked into the cold waters of Cabrillo Beach as seen in this picture of the 1954 swim. In later years, the number grew to one to two thousand people in the water. For 1954, the king was Bob Heron and the queen was Margaret Koch.

King John Truta knights a young boy during the annual Cabrillo Beach Polar Bears Club New Year's Swim in 1955.

After a splash or swim in the brisk water of Cabrillo Beach, participants were invited to a hot cup of tea or hot chocolate as seen in this 1955 photograph. The swimmers, from left to right, are (first row) Jeni Cook, two unidentified women, and John Truta; (second row) Marguerite Gardiner and three unidentified women; (third row) Gregory Zilkov, Norman Plover, and Frenchie Parsons. That year the king was John Truta and the queen was Florench Ferkich.

Joe Hines was a ranger for Cabrillo Camp for many years. Joe and his wife, Olivea, helped coordinate the schedules of the many campers who used the camp.

In 1946, the Los Angeles Area Council of Boy Scouts originally leased what is today called the Cabrillo Beach Youth Waterfront Center property. Located at the base of the cliffs directly below the middle reservation of Fort MacArthur, Cabrillo Camp, as it was then known, catered to both Scouts and other youth groups. Cabrillo Camp was a primitive facility with old military Quonset huts and portable trailers.

In 1987, improvements to the Cabrillo Beach Youth Waterfront Center included a swimming pool, dining center, shop, staff quarters, boathouse, workout facilities, campgrounds, and an amphitheater. The facilities were named the Spielberg Center after Steven Spielberg, who made a significant donation for the improvements. Mr. Spielberg was also an Eagle Scout.

The pergolas at Cabrillo Beach were very popular with families and groups. Their openness allowed a great view of the beach while offering relief from sun and rain.

The last pergola added to Cabrillo Beach was in the middle of the other five. It was the only one with a gas stove, which offered people the opportunity to cook meals as part of their beach parties.

Covered picnic areas called pergolas were added to outer Cabrillo Beach shortly after the opening of the bathhouse. It took many years for the trees, seen newly planted in this picture, to provide shade for beachgoers.

In the 1940s, Los Angeles City Lifeguards started offering special classes to teach rowing to women and girls—something not commonly done in those days.

Los Angeles City Lifeguards taught sailing at Cabrillo Beach in the 1940s and 1950s. In this photograph are, from left to right, Frank Obuljen, George Whitehead, Eddie Whitehead, and an unidentified youth in the training sailboat *Cutty Sark*.

These three men are sailing a homemade skipjack in Los Angeles Harbor in this *c.* 1930 photograph.

The calm waters of San Pedro Bay attracted sailors who wanted to race their sailboats like this race in San Pedro Bay on August 17, 1981.

Model yacht clubs were also attracted to Cabrillo Beach and its relatively calm waters. Often these clubs were precursors to yacht clubs for people with full-sized boats.

Commodore Walter Many of Los Angeles Yacht Club is seen with his special 5-foot "D" boat model. The commodore's boat won first place in a race near the time this picture was taken.

When windsurfing became popular in the 1970s, Cabrillo Beach was the place to go. Among windsurfing enthusiasts, Cabrillo Beach was called "Hurricane Gulch" because of its reliable afternoon breezes. Contests called Windsurfing Enduros have been conducted at Cabrillo Beach and attracted experts and novices alike.

Jet skiers often enjoy the calm waters of inner Cabrillo Beach, where lifeguards have designated an area for them to scoot around the bay. Angel's Gate Lighthouse is on the right, and a large cargo ship is at anchor on the left.

Outer Cabrillo Beach is subject to occasional surf that is popular with surfers including this young man on a boogie board.

After the Cabrillo Marine Museum moved out in 1981, the bathhouse was mostly abandoned and fell into disrepair. The building started to fall apart over the next several years. Thanks to the Cabrillo Beach Polar Bears Club, Cabrillo Beach Boosters, dedicated community members, and the City of Los Angeles, funding was found and plans were made to renovate the venerable building.

The newly renovated Cabrillo Beach Bathhouse was rededicated on October 12, 2002, which was the 70th anniversary of its original opening to the public. On hand for the dedication, starting third from the left in front, are bathhouse recreation director Deanne Dedmon, past Los Angeles City councilman Rudy Svornich, Congresswoman Jane Harmon, Cabrillo Beach Polar Bears Club member Kim White, Los Angeles City councilman Tom LaBonge, Los Angeles City councilwoman Janice Hahn, Cabrillo Marine Museum director emeritus John M. Olguin, and Los Angeles Department of Recreation and Parks general manager Manuel Mollinedo.

Ocean fishing is a passion for many people who come to Cabrillo Beach. California law allows people to fish from man-made structures like piers and breakwaters without a license.

Four

LIFEGUARDS

In 1925, San Pedro was annexed by the City of Los Angeles, and the newly formed Los Angeles City Lifeguards would become responsible for ocean safety at Cabrillo Beach. In the 1930s, competitions started that helped sharpen ocean life-saving skills and promote team unity. The first junior lifeguard programs were also started in the 1930s but would not become an annual program until the program at Cabrillo Beach started in the late 1940s. The City of Los Angeles Ocean Lifeguards merged with the Los Angeles County Lifeguards in 1975. In 1986, city lifeguards returned to providing protection to inner Cabrillo Beach while county lifeguards took responsibility for safety of outer Cabrillo Beach. This condition continues to this day.

Some of the lifeguards of importance at Cabrillo Beach included Myron Cox, who served as a Los Angeles City Lifeguard for a record 42 years, and John M. Olguin, who served as lifeguard captain at Cabrillo Beach even after he took over the directorship of Cabrillo Marine Museum in 1949.

Myron Cox was a City of Los Angeles Lifeguard for a record 42 years. Although he spent most of his time at Venice Beach, he was a regular participant in many events at Cabrillo Beach during his tenure.

The heavy Peterson paddleboard was an important lifesaving tool for lifeguards. Its rounded bottom allowed lifeguards to easily cut through the water on their way to a rescue. Tired swimmers were very happy to be able to hang onto the stable paddleboard.

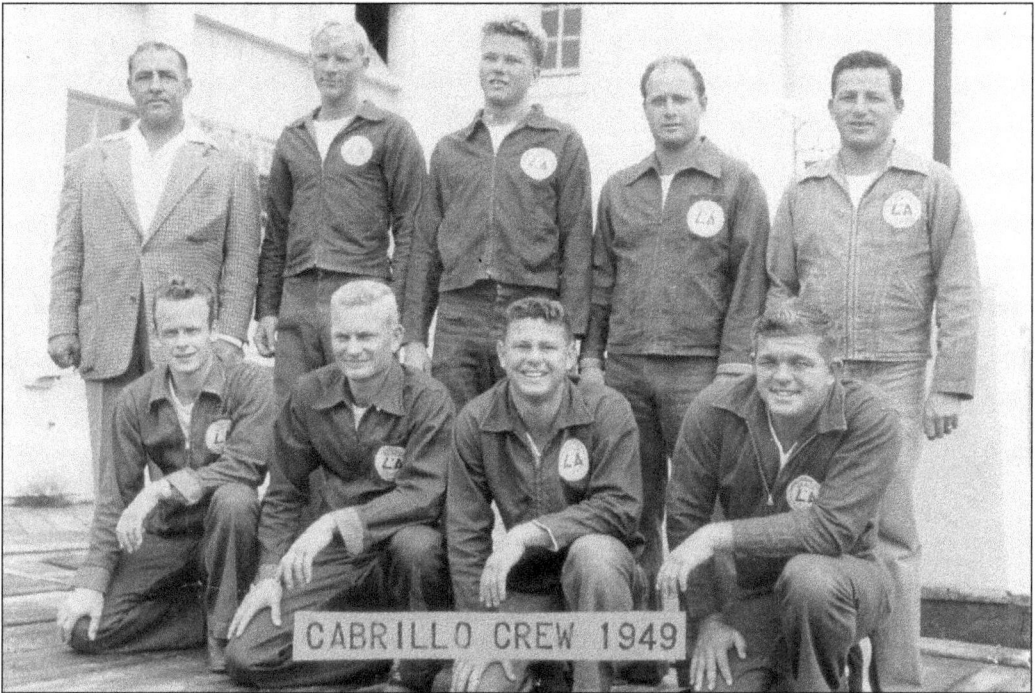

Myron Cox, standing on the far left, was supervisor of lifeguards in 1949. The other lifeguards at Cabrillo Beach are, from left to right, (first row) Donald Krebs, Chancey Hubbard, Joe Alamati, and George Enslow; (second row) Myron Cox, Halleck Robb, Bud Williams, Anthony Tomich, and John M. Olguin.

John M. Olguin started as a lifeguard in 1937 at the age of 16. Captain Olguin continued to spend part of his time as a lifeguard while serving as director of the Cabrillo Marine Museum. During John's lifeguard days, he supervised four of his brothers who were lifeguards at Cabrillo Beach.

Lifeguards pose with their beach dory in 1952. Regular training with the dory was conducted so lifeguards could get in and out of the surf efficiently during rescues. The lifeguards are, from left to right, Leonard Olguin, Albert Olguin, Donald Raskoff, Bill Arendain, Dave Taylor, Donald Landwher, Frank Obuljen, Donald Krebs, Ronnie Mckinon, and Chauncy Hubbard; kneeling in front is Capt. John M. Olguin.

A junior lifeguard program at Cabrillo Beach allowed boys to spend the summer learning the skills necessary to be a lifeguard. The junior lifeguards at Cabrillo Beach were transported to other beaches such as Venice Beach for competitions. Often the contests were referred to as "Battle of the Beach."

Junior lifeguards practiced many skills including the use of paddleboards. This picture shows one of many competitions throughout the year for junior lifeguards.

Competition was an important part of the training for junior lifeguards. Virtually every day they would have an opportunity to show their newly learned skills and push their level of endurance.

Working as a team is an essential skill for junior lifeguards to learn. Getting a rowboat to the water quickly and rowing in unison to the rescue could be the difference between life and death for a swimmer in trouble.

During some of the junior lifeguard sessions, a special program was tried where each junior lifeguard had an adult lifeguard as a mentor. These one-on-one experiences were very successful. Standing on the left is Roy Olguin, and standing on the far right is George Enslow.

The junior lifeguards spent a large portion of their time building strength needed for the job of a lifeguard. Handling the oversized paddleboards was a big task for many of the younger juniors. These boards were also used by the lifeguards to play paddleboard water polo.

In the early days of the junior lifeguard program, only boys were allowed to participate. In the 1980s, girls were welcomed to join.

Pictured here in the early 1950s are Los Angeles City Lifeguard Leonard Olguin and an unidentified woman serving as king and queen at the end of the year potluck banquet for the junior lifeguards.

After a long summer of training and competitions, the junior lifeguards really enjoyed their final banquet. Hats were required to be worn by all in attendance.

Five

CABRILLO MARINE MUSEUM AND CABRILLO MARINE AQUARIUM

The Cabrillo Marine Museum began as a card table filled with shells in front of Bob Foster's lifeguard tower in Venice Beach. In 1935, these specimens were moved to the empty bathhouse at Cabrillo Beach, where a museum was born. Cabrillo Marine Museum opened its doors in the Cabrillo Beach Bathhouse with collections of shells and other local marine life, which expanded to include preserved specimens from other parts of the world and eventually maritime exhibits as well.

In 1981, Cabrillo Marine Museum transformed into the Frank Gehry–designed modern facility focusing exclusively on the great strength of the original museum with its lively programs about Southern California marine life built up over the years by the energy and creativity of director emeritus John Olguin and his many volunteers. Dr. Susanne Lawrenz-Miller, codirector at the time, transformed a traditional museum into a combination museum-aquarium-marine laboratory focusing on Southern California's diverse marine habitats and added field/laboratory programming.

Cabrillo Marine Museum changed its name to Cabrillo Marine Aquarium in 1993. The name change made it clear that the museum displayed a large collection of living Southern California animals and plants surrounded by more traditional museum exhibits to educate visitors.

The most recent expansion opened in 2004 and was designed by Barton Phelps, a protege of Frank Gehry. This expansion added two exhibit halls (the Exploration Center and the Aquatic Nursery), the S. Mark Taper Courtyard, and the Virginia Reid Moore Marine Research Library. With these new public spaces, Cabrillo Marine Aquarium continues to strive to be internationally recognized as a leader in providing friendly and accessible seashore programs and facilities for understanding and improving the relationship people have with the marine environment.

The first floor of the Cabrillo Beach Bathhouse was filled with displays of marine life. These exhibits varied but included the largest collection of West Coast snails on display anywhere.

Neatly labeled and catalogued, these shells documented subtidal variations on snails from San Diego to the Oregon border. In addition, shells from around the world highlighted many colorful and unique adaptations.

The Cabrillo Beach Bathhouse's second floor was converted from a dance hall to maritime exhibit space. In 1981, the maritime exhibits were moved into the ferry building on Harbor Boulevard near downtown San Pedro and renamed the Los Angeles Maritime Museum.

Dr. William Lloyd was appointed the first director in 1935. He was a retired dentist who had a great love for nature and happily improvised what was needed to make museum exhibits. The owner of the Cabrillo Café saved one-gallon mayonnaise jars that Dr. Lloyd would later use to preserve specimens. For years, Cabrillo Marine Museum was informally known as the "Cabrillo Mayonnaise Jar Museum."

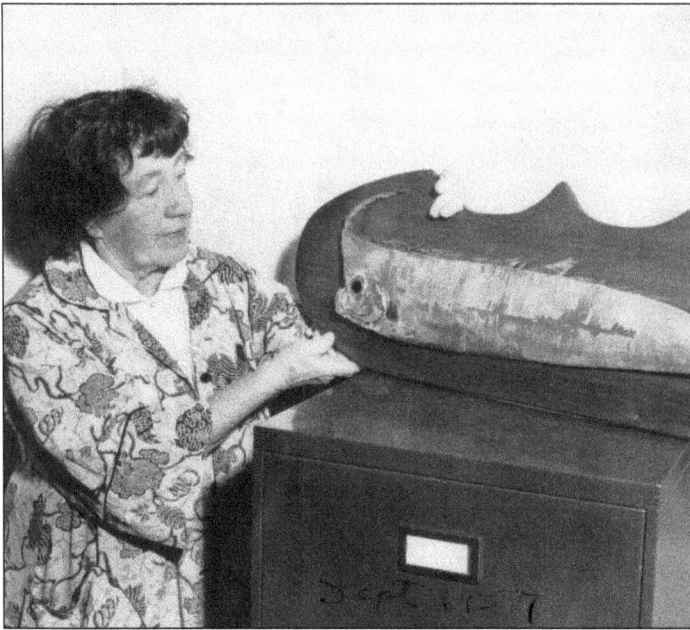

Beatrice Hess was responsible for many of the fish and other marine life specimens adorning the walls of Cabrillo Marine Museum in the Cabrillo Beach Bathhouse. In this picture, Ms. Hess poses with one of her mounts.

Some of the early staff of the Cabrillo Marine Museum included lifeguard John M. Olguin, who would help Dr. Lloyd at the Museum when he was not on duty. In the picture from left to right are John M. Olguin, Don ?, Marge ?, John Truta, and unidentified.

Grunion have been spawning at Cabrillo Beach since its creation in 1928. In 1951, John Olguin began the grunion programs and developed his famous "Do It! Do It!" teaching style in which visitors dance and sing.

The mounted fish displayed in the first floor of the Cabrillo Marine Museum were donated by local fisherman and prepared and mounted on the walls. The mounts provided examples of the many shapes and sizes of Southern California fish.

Tours of the Cabrillo Marine Museum were so popular with local schools that many had to be turned away. In the 1960s, director Olguin tried hosting some spring tours out on the beach. These new programs enabled more students to be involved than could fit into the small confines of the bathhouse.

The spring program was said to take advantage of the largest classroom in the world—the Pacific Ocean. Bright colorful banners make for a festive feel to the docent stations on the beach, where school children learned about ocean life. Angel's Gate Lighthouse can be seen in the upper right in addition to a bait barge in San Pedro Bay.

On spring and early summer evenings, grunion use the sand of Cabrillo Beach as a place to spawn, depositing their eggs in the sand. Since the early 1950s, Cabrillo Marine Museum (later the Cabrillo Marine Aquarium) has welcomed visitors to watch this amazing natural phenomenon at Meet the Grunion programs.

Along with John Olguin (kneeling and dressed in black) and his wife, Muriel (kneeling and dressed in white), the group at this run included Muriel's father, California State Fish and Game captain Clarence Groat (standing on the far right in the hat). For the first time, on this night, Olguin invited the public to watch the grunion run on Cabrillo Beach.

Cabrillo Marine Museum invited people to learn about grunion by showing them a movie about the life history of these unusual fish. Large groups of people sat on carpet spread over the sidewalk in front of Cabrillo Marine Museum to watch the film on a white sheet hanging above the entrance. After seeing the movie and braving the cold and damp weather, people walked around the bathhouse and were treated to seeing the grunion running on outer Cabrillo Beach.

Director John Olguin began teaching volunteers to be docents for the Cabrillo Marine Museum in 1973. This training continues as docents help teach schoolchildren visiting Cabrillo Marine Aquarium about the wonders of the ocean. Nini Buchheim, later to become the Cabrillo Marine Museum gift shop manager, is in the middle front of this photograph (without sunglasses).

In the early days of free school tours, director John Olguin greeted the students in front of Cabrillo Marine Museum. He would use the ship's capstan installed there to illustrate the physical advantage the machine would give sailors aboard a ship in hauling in lines. He had many of the larger students hang onto a line wound around the capstan and to hold their ground. Meanwhile, it took only one of the smaller students to easily turn the capstan and pull in the line with the larger students in tow.

In the early 1970s, the bathhouse was becoming too small to accommodate the demand for school tours. The City of Los Angeles came up with a plan and funding for a new Cabrillo Marine Museum. Early plans called for the new building to be constructed just west of the bathhouse on outer Cabrillo Beach. Residents of San Pedro were very much against this plan and a new site was chosen next to the cliffs on inner Cabrillo Beach. Those at the ground-breaking ceremony on February 11, 1974, from left to right, are (first row) Arthur Almeida, Frances Botwin, Barbara Bechler, Wynn Jewers, Bob Beck, Marji Frank, and Greg Smith; (second row) Dr. Jack Menzie, Robert Goldstone, and Bill Samaras; (third row) John M. Olguin.

The skeleton of the new Cabrillo Marine Museum takes shape in 1974 across the parking lot from the bathhouse and up against the cliff.

Architect Frank Gehry and associates came up with a design for the new Cabrillo Marine Museum. Mr. Gehry's vision was for the building to fit in with the harbor, so he liberally used chain-link fencing, stucco, and galvanized-steel plating and posts. He also wanted to give it the feel of a campus with different buildings and a central courtyard. The plan included a 300-seat auditorium, 7,500-square-foot exhibit hall, administration building, marine lab and classroom, research lab, and exhibit preparation space.

In 1974, Dr. Susanne Lawrenz-Miller was hired by the City of Los Angeles Recreation and Parks Department to develop the plans for the exhibits in the new Cabrillo Marine Museum. Dr. Lawrenz-Miller recruited eminent marine scientists in Southern California who together helped her develop the exhibit plan that is still in place to this day.

Los Angeles city mayor Tom Bradley attended the opening ceremony of the new Cabrillo Marine Museum on October 21, 1981. Codirectors Dr. Susanne Lawrenz-Miller and John M. Olguin were the masters of ceremonies.

Los Angeles mayor Tom Bradley had the honor of cutting the ribbon at the opening of the new Cabrillo Marine Museum on October 21, 1981.

World-renowned architect Frank Gehry designed the new Cabrillo Marine Museum. Frank said he designed the courtyard and auditorium with gregarious teacher and codirector John M. Olguin in mind. For the exhibit hall, Gehry's thoughts turned to studious scientist and codirector Dr. Susanne Lawrenz-Miller. Today the auditorium bears John's name, and the exhibit hall is named after Susanne.

Attendees at the opening ceremonies for the new Cabrillo Marine Museum on October 21, 1981, helped transfer seawater from the tanks in the bathhouse to the tanks in the new facility by being part of a coffee-can bucket brigade.

Longtime chief aquarist Lloyd Ellis (center of photograph with glasses) directs coffee can brigade participants in filling the first aquarium tank with seawater at the new Cabrillo Marine Museum on opening day. The City of Los Angeles mayor had the honor of dumping the first coffee can full of seawater into the aquarium tank.

In 1981, the San Pedro Municipal Ferry Building, Los Angeles Historic-Cultural Monument No. 146, became the home of the Los Angeles Maritime Museum. The building was constructed in 1941 and was home to the ferry that carried cars and people between San Pedro and Terminal Island. The ferry service closed in 1963 at about the time the Vincent Thomas Bridge was opened to the public.

On July 12, 2002, Cabrillo Marine Aquarium broke ground on a $10-million expansion. Funding was about $7 million from public sources (state, county, and city bond measures passed by the voters) for the building and about $3 million from the FRIENDS of Cabrillo Marine Aquarium for the exhibits. Taking the ceremonial first shovels of dirt from left to right are Gary DeLong, exhibits director Mike Schaadt, capital campaign director Suzanne Campi, City of Los Angeles councilwoman Janice Hahn, director emeritus John M. Olguin, Los Angeles mayor James Hahn, California state assemblywoman Betty Karnette, director Susanne Lawrenz-Miller, FRIENDS of Cabrillo Marine Aquarium chairman Dan Mueller, and programs director Larry Fukuhara.

The skeleton of the expansion building starts to take shape just south of the John M. Olguin Auditorium in this 2003 picture. The primary reason for expanding Cabrillo Marine Aquarium was to accommodate more schoolchildren on free tours.

Dr. Susanne Lawrenz-Miller led the opening ceremonies for the expansion to Cabrillo Marine Aquarium in 2004. Seated on the podium from left to right are Department of Recreation and Parks assistant general manager George Stigile, Recreation and Parks representative Ron Deaton, chairman of the board of FRIENDS of Cabrillo Marine Aquarium Jack Ferrell, and director emeritus John M. Olguin.

The official opening of the expansion to Cabrillo Marine Aquarium on October 23, 2004, featured a cutting of a ribbon of kelp. Participants at the cutting, from left to right, are aquarist Lisa Bartley, exhibits director Mike Schaadt, exhibits curator Ed Mastro, director emeritus John M. Olguin, City of Los Angeles Department of Recreation and Parks representative Ron Deaton, California State assemblywoman Betty Karnette, director Dr. Susanne Lawrenz-Miller, City of Los Angeles councilwoman Janice Hahn, junior volunteer Shelby Tsuji, Department of Recreation and Parks assistant general manager George Stigile, S. Mark Taper Foundation representative Ray Reisler, Virginia Reid Moore family representative Capt. Charles Moore, and architect Barton Phelps.

On opening day, the expansion spaces were crowded with visitors and well-wishers. The expansion enabled Cabrillo Marine Aquarium to serve more schoolchildren with education about Southern California marine life.

Junior and senior high school docents added to the festive feel of the opening-day festivities by welcoming the crowd dressed up as marine animals. The names of the students from left to right are two unidentified individuals, Elizabeth Cawley, and Jerome Cawley. The students are standing in front of the signature architectural element of the front of the expansion.

Longtime Cabrillo Marine Museum volunteer Horace Staubley, also known as "Bubble Man," kept schoolchildren entertained while they waited for their turn for a tour.

Six

EVENTS

Different significant and memorable events have taken place at Cabrillo Beach over the years. Some have happened as acts of nature like the storms of 1932, 1933, 1939, 1940, and 1946. A very large leatherback turtle was harpooned off Point Fermin and was used to make a mold for the model on display at Cabrillo Marine Aquarium.

The popularity of Cabrillo Beach as a community gathering place is clear from the events that have take place over the years, such as Fourth of July celebrations, San Juan Days, Filipino Festivals, and even a visit by the Great White Fleet in 1908.

Staff at Cabrillo Marine Museum joined with local community members in reenacting historical events significant to San Pedro and Southern California. In his book *Two Years before the Mast*, Richard Henry Dana wrote about cowhides being thrown off the cliffs at San Pedro and taken to waiting boats to be used for trade in the 1830s. This event was reenacted at the cliffs above Cabrillo Beach for a few years in the early 1950s. Staff at Cabrillo Marine Museum also joined with the community to reenact the landing of Juan Rodriguez Cabrillo in Southern California. It was staged at Cabrillo Beach in the early days and was eventually moved to San Miguel Island, the actual place historians believe the landing took place.

Other popular community events held at Cabrillo Beach over the years included model-ship races, small-sailboat regattas, and bodybuilding contests.

The Cabrillo Marine Museum (later Aquarium) also sponsored many community events like Autumn Sea Fair, Whale Fiesta, the 10-kilometer Grunion Run, Chocolate Lobster Dive, Earth Day, and Coastal Cleanup Day.

Man-made disasters have also taken place like the explosion of the Liberian tanker *Sansinea* in 1976.

In 1938, the fishing boat *Izu* out of San Pedro harbor harpooned a leatherback turtle off Point Fermin that weighed in at 1,100 pounds.

The turtle measured 38 inches across, 88 inches from head to tail, and was so heavy that the boat listed as it was hauled up by a winch. It was transported to a professional model maker, so a mold could be made to make a model to exhibit.

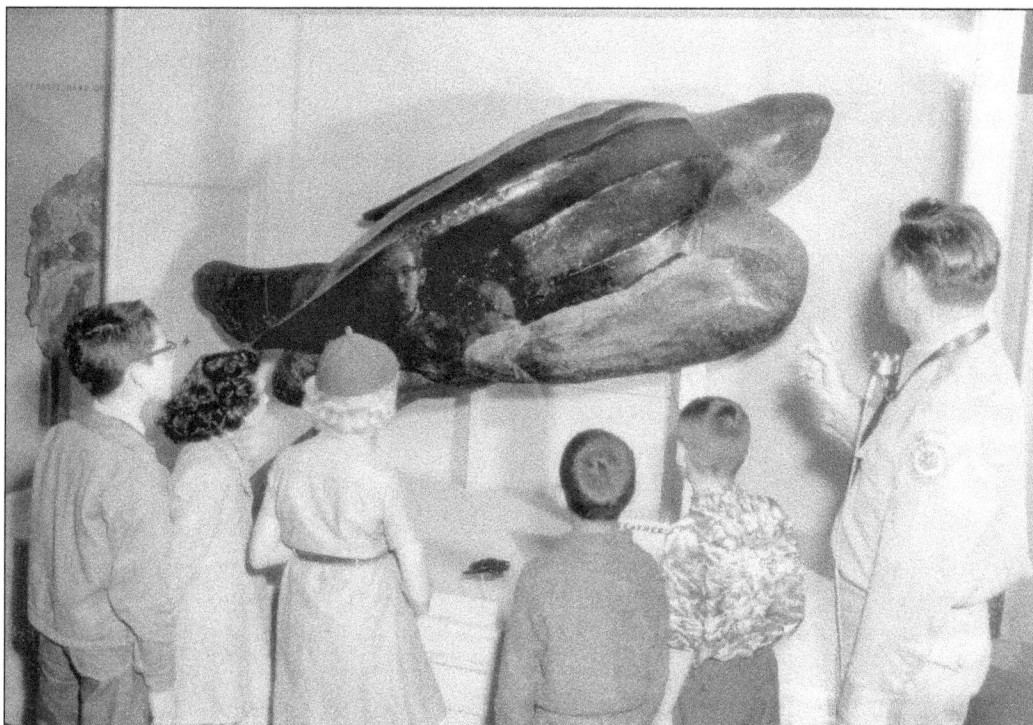

The leatherback turtle model on display at the Cabrillo Marine Museum and the Cabrillo Marine Aquarium was made from a mold of the turtle on the previous page.

Beach cleanups like this one in 1989 were organized by the Cabrillo Marine Museum staff who invited the public to join them in keeping Cabrillo Beach free of trash.

People participate regularly in beach cleanups at Cabrillo Beach. Much of the trash originates from inland communities and is brought via the storm drainage system to the ocean where it accumulates on the shoreline.

Earth Day events start out with an early morning beach cleanup, which is very well attended. Each cleanup ends with a tally for the total number of items picked up and a total weight of the trash. Tons of trash have been picked up by volunteers over the years.

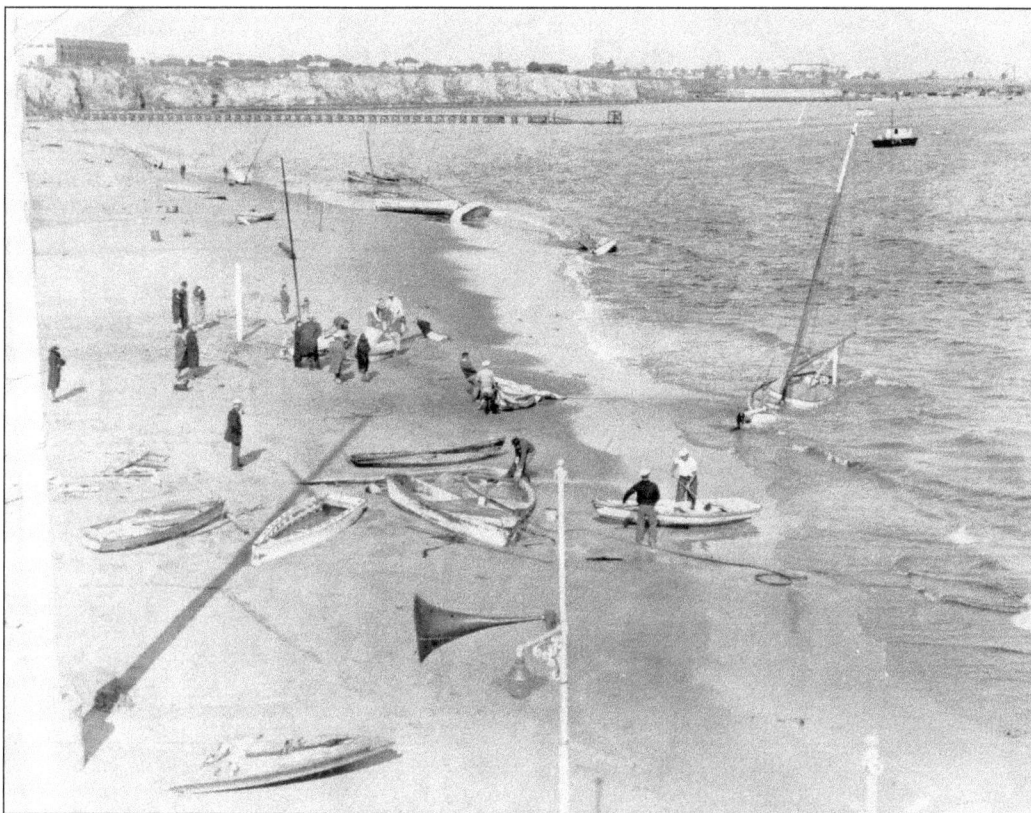

Over the years, storms have had dramatic impacts on San Pedro Bay and Cabrillo Beach. This storm in December of 1932 resulted in many small crafts being washed up onto inner Cabrillo Beach.

Heavy storms in January of 1933 caused a great deal of damage to vessels like this sailboat.

The storms in January of 1933 caused heavy damage to the pier of the boathouse at inner Cabrillo Beach.

Erosion of the beach during these massive Pacific storms was significant, as can be seen in this picture taken on September 27, 1939, of outer Cabrillo Beach looking towards Point Fermin.

Beach erosion after a storm in January of 1940 eventually led to the U.S. Army Corps of Engineers' decision to replenish outer Cabrillo Beach.

People flocked to outer Cabrillo Beach to watch the force of storm waves. Los Angeles City Lifeguards were busy keeping the crowds at a safe distance.

The storm in November of 1946 caused the death of one person and 22 boats to be washed up onto inner Cabrillo Beach.

Summer days always draw a crowd to Cabrillo Beach. One of the busiest summer days is the Fourth of July. The parking lot and inner Cabrillo Beach are packed as beachgoers escape warmer temperatures inland. In the foreground of this picture is the sewer pipe that carried sewage away from the busy beach area. The Sower House can be seen on the far right.

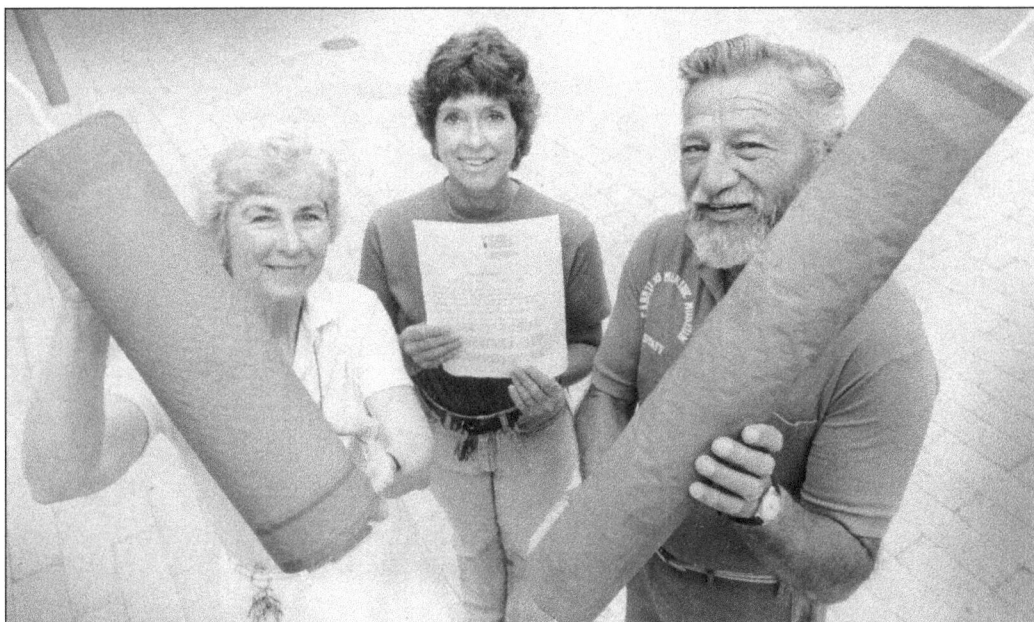

In 1950, John M. Olguin began an annual campaign to raise money for the fireworks at the Fourth of July celebration at Cabrillo Beach. Thanks to John's Herculean efforts, fireworks have been part of the day's events for many years and will continue to be for years to come. John is joined in this picture with longtime Cabrillo Marine Museum volunteer coordinator Marji Frank (left) and volunteer Anne Holmes (center).

Cabrillo Beach was just as packed with people at night on the Fourth of July as during the day. Everyone stayed for the show in the night sky and looked forward to the grand finale, when many fireworks were sent into the air at the same time.

Los Angeles City Fire Department Fire Boat No. 2, the *Ralph J. Scott*, joins in the fun at a 1980s Fourth of July celebration by showing off its water cannons just off inner Cabrillo Beach.

Los Angeles City Fire Department's new Fireboat No. 2, which went into service in 2003, demonstrates its water cannons at the Fourth of July celebration just off inner Cabrillo Beach.

For a few years in the early 1950s, staff from Cabrillo Marine Museum reenacted the practice of throwing cowhides from the cliffs described by Richard Henry Dana in his book *Two Years Before the Mast*. In this picture, the person in the white hat on the left is Fr. Patrick McPoland, who plays the part of the Roman Catholic priest from the San Gabriel Mission. He is bargaining with the captain of the *Pilgrim*, played here by Ray Wallis, about the price to pay for the hides.

Actors dressed as Native Americans rehearse prior to performing the first Landing of Cabrillo pageant in 1936. Chairman of the pageant Ernest Ehrke is dressed in a Spanish costume. Longtime city lifeguard Myron Cox is dressed as the Native American kneeling in the middle of the group.

Before the 1936 reenactment of the landing of Juan Rodriguez Cabrillo, San Pedro had a pageant celebrating the explorer, which included a parade in downtown San Pedro.

In this San Pedro Chamber of Commerce publicity picture from 1936, a man dressed as Juan Rodriguez Cabrillo has swimsuit-clad admirers at Cabrillo Beach.

The landing reenactment always has the famous explorer claiming the new land for King Carlos of Spain and includes a blessing of the endeavor by a priest.

The 50th anniversary of the reenactment of the landing of Juan Rodriguez Cabrillo took place in 1986. For this special celebration, John M. Olguin's son John Rodriguez Cabrillo Olguin (left) portrayed Juan Rodriguez Cabrillo. It was an Olguin family affair as John portrayed the priest (second from the left) and John's grandson Micah Olguin was cast as a conquistador (second from the right).

Since the mid-1970s, the reenactment also took place on San Miguel Island, the most remote of the Channel Islands chain and where Cabrillo was reported to have made his first landing. The island is also one of the reported places of his grave. Cabrillo Marine Museum director emeritus John M. Olguin, dressed as the famous conquistador explorer, has been involved in this reenactment since it started in 1936.

The Liberian bulk tanker SS *Sansinea* is seen here at berth No. 46 across from inner Cabrillo Beach in 1963.

In 1976, the SS *Sansinea* exploded while tied at berth No. 46. The explosion blew out many harbor-facing windows in San Pedro and could be heard more than 25 miles away.

The crude oil that spilled from SS *Sansinea* spread throughout inner Cabrillo Beach and the San Pedro Breakwater. It took cleanup crews weeks to remove the oil. Biologists from California State University at Long Beach conducted studies to document the long-term effects on the local ecosystem.

Cabrillo Beach can be seen in the background during the mass funeral ceremonies held at Trona Field, Middle Reservation of Fort MacArthur, in San Pedro for the 48 naval officers and enlisted men who perished in the main battery turret explosion aboard the battleship USS *Mississippi*. The men were asphyxiated as a result of an explosion in the No. 2 main battery turret during gunnery practice off San Pedro on June 12, 1924.

With the help of biologists such as Bill Samaras and John Heyning from the American Cetacean Society, Cabrillo Marine Museum codirector John M. Olguin organized people to make a full-scale sculpture of different species of whales at the annual Whale Fiesta like this one on outer Cabrillo Beach in 1980.

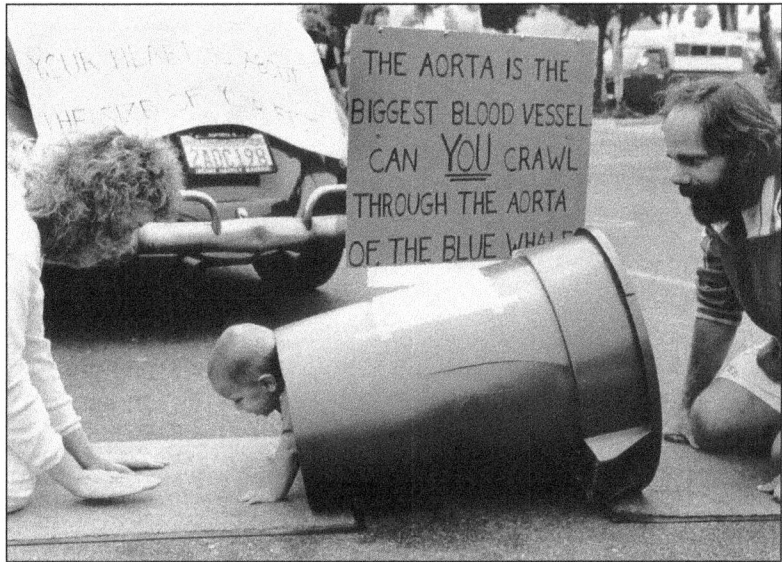

Exhibits at the Whale Fiesta helped people understand the ways whales were similar to humans and the ways they were different. Exhibits curator Ed Mastro demonstrates to the crowd just how large the aorta is in a blue whale by having his young son Steven crawl to his wife, Lisa Mastro, through a plastic trash can with the lid removed.

The endeavor of making the sand-sculpture whale took all day and included an interactive lecture by Cabrillo Marine Museum director John M. Olguin. He had participants stand to make an outline of a whale and show how it eats by having some people play the plankton going in the open mouth to be eaten. It was a great view from the Goodyear blimp. After John's retirement in 1986, Cabrillo Marine Museum programs director Larry Fukuhara organized the event that continues to this day.

The Whale Fiesta ended with a feast of watermelons for all present. Volunteers and staff were very appreciative of the treat after a daylong struggle with shaping sand into a full-sized depiction of a whale.

Puerto Rican heritage was celebrated at Cabrillo Beach during San Juan Day like this one held in the 1960s. This event was eventually moved to Long Beach.

President Carter designated 1980 as the "Year of the Coast." The Cabrillo Marine Museum joined in efforts to make people aware of the changes along the coastline and the need for public participation in decisions to protect the coast.

In 1907, Pres. Theodore Roosevelt sent 16 new battleships painted white on an around-the-world cruise to show American sea power. Some people called it "gunboat diplomacy." The Great White Fleet made a stop at San Pedro in April of 1908.

Sailboat races became popular shortly after the San Pedro Breakwater created quiet waters for the smaller sailors to take advantage. The Mercury National Championship took place in August of 1981 and was sponsored by the Cabrillo Beach Yacht Club.

This regatta was held in the early days of Cabrillo Beach. These two small sailboats are headed for the end of the pier of the boathouse.

Small boats came into their own at Cabrillo Beach when the City of Los Angeles Department of Playground and Recreation staged a regatta for small craft off of the Cabrillo Boathouse in the 1930s. It was a feature of the annual regatta staged by the Civic Regatta Association off Point Fermin.

Sailing events were held in the waters off Cabrillo Beach at the 1932 Summer Olympics in Los Angeles. The boathouse and bathhouse at Cabrillo Beach were staging areas for these events. In this picture, Colin Ratsey's Star Class sailboat *Joy* passes in front of the Angel's Gate Lighthouse. Ratsey took second place for Great Britain in this race.

Known as the Pan-American Flying Clippers, seaplanes of the mid-1900s made landings and takeoffs at Cabrillo Beach. On July 27, 1940, the *Honolulu Clipper* made a visit. Cabrillo Beach lifeguard John M. Olguin can be seen on the paddleboard below the left wing of the plane.

The *American Clipper* made its first flight to New Zealand via San Pedro in the late 1930s.

The *Yankee Clipper* visited Cabrillo Beach on its way to San Francisco on March 30, 1935. Many of these seaplanes were sold to the U.S. Navy and Army, but after the war few were put back into civilian service, and by the 1950s all were scrapped.

Swimmers are a hearty bunch at Cabrillo Beach as evidenced by this picture taken by John M. Olguin of two ladies out for a swim on a rainy day in early February of 1958. Jeni is on the right and ? Marshall is on the left. Cook braved the cold winter temperatures at Cabrillo Beach for many years.

Cabrillo Beach has been a common target for people swimming across the channel from Catalina Island to the mainland. Here Ray Carmassi is swimming across, with his trainer rowing alongside for safety, in 1952.

Shortly after the opening of the new Cabrillo Marine Museum in 1981, the public was invited to join in a 10-kilometer race called the Grunion Run. Organizers that year from left to right were Emmy Reeves, John M. Olguin, and Kathy Haynes. Tom Lacey (not pictured) of San Pedro was also instrumental in organizing the run.

Although it only lasted a few years, the race was another way Cabrillo Marine Museum involved the community in activities at Cabrillo Beach.

In the 1980s, Cabrillo Beach was the site of local bodybuilding contests that featured men and women. John Burch, who owned a gym in San Pedro, was one of the organizers along with the City of Los Angeles Department of Recreation and Parks and the Los Angeles County Department of Parks and Recreation.

Sailors from ships at anchor in San Pedro Bay would often take a shoreboat to Navy Pier near what is now the youth camp on the northern end of Cabrillo Beach.

Divers have come to Cabrillo Beach for scuba diving since the beginning of the sport. This is a picture of Chauncey Hubbard using Aqua-Lung gear at inner Cabrillo Beach next to the boathouse pier.

In 1997, FRIENDS of Cabrillo Marine Aquarium invited divers to come to Cabrillo Beach to search for shrink-wrapped chocolate lobster tails planted in the shallow waters of outer Cabrillo Beach.

Dr. Robert Given was an instrumental volunteer at Chocolate Lobster Dive by reciting the rules and officially starting the dive.

In the later years of the Chocolate Lobster Dive, there were over 400 divers joining in the fun. Many of the chocolate lobsters contained a number for a prize that was redeemable at the completion of the dive.

For the last couple years of the event, different colored plaster molds of lobster tails were planted and redeemed for chocolate lobster tails and prizes. Cabrillo Marine Aquarium staffers also joined in the fun as seen here with aquarist Eric Forsman (left) and exhibits director Mike Schaadt. The annual event was a fund-raiser for educational programs and was discontinued in 2005, when it was decided that the work to put on the event was not worth the money raised.

In July 1996, scenes from the film *Slappy and the Stinkers* were shot at Cabrillo Marine Aquarium. The movie was directed by Barnet Kellman and starred B. D. Wong and Bronson Pinchot.

Just before the renovation of the bathhouse, it was used as a location for scenes in the 1997 movie *Face Off*, which was directed by John Woo and starred John Travolta and Nicholas Cage. The bathhouse was made to resemble a church in Mexico.

Cabrillo Beach has always welcomed visitors. The City of Los Angeles Department of Recreation and Parks and the Los Angeles County Department of Parks and Recreation have strived throughout the history of Cabrillo Beach to make it a safe, fun, and educational destination for the residents

of Los Angeles. This group of Job's Daughters poses for a picture at Cabrillo Beach in 1927, and they show the simple joy a place like this can bring to people.

ACROSS AMERICA, PEOPLE ARE DISCOVERING SOMETHING WONDERFUL. *THEIR HERITAGE.*

Arcadia Publishing is the leading local history publisher in the United States. With more than 4,000 titles in print and hundreds of new titles released every year, Arcadia has extensive specialized experience chronicling the history of communities and celebrating America's hidden stories, bringing to life the people, places, and events from the past. To discover the history of other communities across the nation, please visit:

www.arcadiapublishing.com

Customized search tools allow you to find regional history books about the town where you grew up, the cities where your friends and family live, the town where your parents met, or even that retirement spot you've been dreaming about.

MAP SEARCH